Was It Worth It?

PURPOSEFUL PARENTING PLAN WORKBOOK

Carol Jean Wilson Allen

Copyright © 2025 by Carol Jean Wilson Allen

All rights reserved. No part of this book may be reproduced in any manner whatsoever without written permission except in the case of brief quotations embodied in critical articles and reviews.

ISBN: 9781950544578

Rand-Smith Publishing

WORKBOOK

Tip: You can tape your own photo here for inspiration!

Welcome!

This workbook is designed to complement the strategies outlined in my book **Was It Worth It?** and guide you in creating your own Purposeful Parenting Plan (PPP). Based on real-life experiences and thoughtful reflections, the workbook offers practical exercises and prompts to help you customize these overarching strategies to fit your unique family dynamics.

As you engage with each section, you are encourage to reflect on your parenting journey, identifying the values, principles, and approaches that resonate most with you. This process empowers you to embrace the joys and challenges of raising children while ensuring you nurture your own well-being. The workbook is not just a tool for planning—it is an opportunity to learn, adapt, and grow alongside your children.

In addition to providing space for reflection and goal-setting, this workbook emphasizes the importance of open communication, self-awareness, and mindful decision-making. The insights gathered from my personal experiences demonstrate the lifelong impact of intentional parenting in my life. I challenge you to explore these strategies, adapting them to your needs while fostering stronger bonds within your family through this process.

Whether you are a parent, grandparent, or caregiver, this workbook supports your efforts to create a nurturing environment where children thrive and family relationships deepen. As you chart your path, may you find fulfillment in knowing that you are shaping the future with love, care, and purpose.

Let's get started!

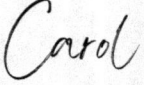

What is a Purposeful Parenting Plan?

In case you have not yet read my book **Was It Worth It?** or if you need a refresher, I'll briefly summarize what a Purposeful Parenting Plan is and then how to begin creating one of your own.

Before you start writing anything down, you should learn the PPP concepts so that you can apply them as you go along. I've broken them down into four areas. Once you understand this section, you will be ready to begin preparing your plan.

The approaches of the Purposeful Parenting Plan are:

- Know Thyself
- Develop the Plan
- Execute the Plan
- Get Feedback

Know Thyself

Parenting is one of the most profound and vital journeys you'll ever embark on, and it begins with a deep, honest exploration of yourself. This isn't a time for judgment or self-criticism but an opportunity to embrace your authentic self. By stripping away blame and expectations, you can understand how you respond to life's challenges, what fuels your energy, and what brings you joy. Whether you thrive on structure or spontaneity, solitude or social connection, your unique traits and preferences shape the way you navigate the highs and lows of life. This personal reflection is your chance to uncover the core of who you are and, in turn, create a parenting style that aligns with your true self.

This journey of self-discovery is a treasure map to successful and fulfilling parenting. By knowing yourself—your passions, needs, and the rhythms that bring you peace—you can better understand how to guide and nurture your children. Embrace the process with excitement, knowing that getting to know yourself is key to becoming the best parent you can be. This is your moment to celebrate the extraordinary person you are and to step confidently into your role, ready to support your children in a way that feels genuine, balanced, and joyful.

Write down a few of your qualities here. We'll go into more depth later.

_____

_____

_____

_____

Examples: easy going, structured, decisive, lenient, confident, etc.

Develop the Plan

Developing a Purposeful Parenting Plan (PPP) begins with intentionality and self-awareness. While parenting can feel like an unpredictable journey, having a thoughtful plan helps you navigate it with confidence and clarity. Just as strategic plans guide successful organizations, knowing your vision, goals, strengths, and weaknesses will empower you to make mindful decisions for your family. The sooner you understand yourself, the sooner you can craft a PPP that aligns with your unique reality. By applying proven strategies like identifying strengths, acknowledging limitations, and recognizing opportunities and challenges, you equip yourself to handle parenting with purpose and resilience.

Parenting is not a solo mission—it's a team effort. Recognizing where you need support and leaning on others can be transformative. Life's obstacles are inevitable, but with a clear plan, you can face them with courage and adaptability. Think of your PPP as a way to harness all the knowledge, experience, and wisdom you've gathered, transforming it into meaningful action. So, embrace this journey of self-discovery and strategic planning with enthusiasm. Together, with love, support, and a well-prepared plan, you'll navigate the adventure of parenting like the superhero you truly are!

Write down a few members of your support team.

_____

_____

_____

_____

Examples: parents, relatives, family friends, etc.

Execute the Plan

This is it—the moment where all your preparation comes to life! The path ahead, from your child's first days to adulthood, is where your Purposeful Parenting Plan transforms from intention to action. Day by day, as you put your goals into practice, you're building a foundation of love, guidance, and consistency. While it might seem overwhelming at first, trust that your dedication and thoughtful planning will make the journey smoother and more rewarding. Each challenge you tackle and each milestone you celebrate brings you closer to raising confident, capable children and growing stronger as a parent.

You are in control, steering your family toward a life filled with purpose and fulfillment. Your PPP is more than just a plan—it's your roadmap to success and a testament to the love and care you pour into your parenting. Embrace every moment with confidence, knowing that the work you're doing makes a meaningful, lifelong impact. Stay committed, stay inspired, and remember to celebrate your progress. This is your time to shine, and the rewards of this incredible adventure will be worth every effort. Keep going, keep growing—you've got this!

Write down a few ideas about what your plan might look like.

_____
_____
_____
_____
_____

Examples: daily routine, life lessons, short and long-term goals, etc.

Collect Feedback

Gathering feedback from family members, particularly your children, is a valuable way to evaluate and refine your parenting approach. To begin, schedule intentional moments for these discussions. If distance is an issue, consider virtual meetings through platforms like Zoom to make communication more accessible and personal. Ask thoughtful, open-ended questions that invite your children or relatives to share their experiences. Inquire about which aspects of your parenting they found supportive, which they found challenging, and whether they feel equipped to handle life's challenges. By fostering a relaxed, positive atmosphere filled with warmth and humor, you create a safe space where they can speak candidly. It's important to listen with an open mind, free from guilt or judgment, and remain confident in the efforts you've made as a parent.

Recognize that each person may have different perceptions of their upbringing, and these diverse experiences can highlight the strengths and areas for improvement in your parenting style. Reflect on the insights they share and take note of recurring themes or patterns. Pay attention to what worked well and where adjustments might be beneficial. Afterward, use this feedback to refine your plan. Keeping your plan adaptable based on your family's input ensures it remains effective and aligned with your children's evolving needs. Engaging in these conversations not only strengthens your parenting but also deepens your connection with your family members.

Write down a list of people you would like to "interview."

_____

_____

_____

_____

Examples: parents, children, grandchildren, family friends, etc.

Let's Get Started

Now it's time to put those elements into practice to create your own plan.

Over the next few pages you will be guided through each steps with helpful examples and prompts.

Use those as guides to get started on your own unique plan.

REMEMBER!
I'm giving you ideas and guidance, but the content should be yours and yours alone.

Tape your own pic here!

Step 1 – Know Thyself

The first step that we reviewed is to "know thy self," which means clearly understanding where you are in your life and what you want for yourself, personally and professionally. It's going to be a challenge to plan for your children if you haven't made your own plans first, the primary one being that you are prepared to accept the responsibility of being a parent.

When preparing to have children, it's essential to realize that life will change; it will be different. Life will have a new definition. Having children will be a life sentence, but in a good way! Get ready to become another person, to some extent, another version of yourself. If you are realistic about the inevitable changes to your life, it will help you to acclimate. It is better not to focus on the changes that might be interpreted as unfavorable because there will be so many positive lifestyle changes that can result from having a family. Parenthood will usher in new life experiences that can be just as wonderful as your childless life, if not more so.

What changes am I **willing** to make?

_____

_____

_____

_____

Examples: manage shopping sprees, seek flexible work hours, etc.

Know Thyself

Are there some things I am **not willing** to change?

_____

_____

_____

_____

Examples: personal health, career goals, etc.

What type of life do I want to lead once the child is born?

_____

_____

_____

_____

Examples: remain social, take my child everywhere, enlist help, etc.

Know Thyself

When you begin crafting your plan, it's essential to start by gathering all the relevant information. You may have already collected valuable insights during your self-assessment and research phases. Now, it's time to organize this wealth of data effectively.

First, don't worry too much about the format or topics; jot down your ideas and see what you get. You can always go back and finesse them if you like.

Here are mine:
- I am a fighter.
- I will never give up.
- I am a hard worker.
- I observe.
- I listen to other people.
- I am more objective than emotional.
- I plan for the worst and hope for the best.
- I try to avoid making the mistakes that other people make.
- I am a planner.
- I want to incorporate all I am into a plan for raising children.

Now list some characteristics used to describe you. There are no right or wrong answers.

_____
_____
_____
_____
_____

Know Thyself

Get Organized

Once you've chosen your format, it's time to decide on your organizational style. Your style can be as casual or as detailed as you like. Some prefer to write things out in complete sentences, while others like using to-do lists. Here are examples of contrasting approaches.

Casual Style with Bulleted Lists: If you prefer a more relaxed and straightforward approach, create a parenting plan using bulleted lists. You can jot down key points, ideas, and goals in a simple, easy-to-read format. This style is great for busy parents who want to keep things concise. Something like this:

- Morning routine
- Breakfast together
- School drop-off
- Playtime
- Evening routine
- Homework
- Dinner as a family
- Bedtime story

Detailed Style with Headings and Objectives: For those who appreciate structure and thorough planning, use headings, objectives, goals, outlines, and even references to parenting resources. This style allows for comprehensive planning and a deep understanding of your parenting approach.

Whatever method you choose, remember that you can always switch gears if it's not working for you. Try one way and then another until you find a comfortable approach that fits your lifestyle.

Know Thyself

A Balanced Plan
If you're not sure how to begin, start with a basic scenario. Create a realistic routine that fosters both academic growth and quality family time. Start with the age-appropriate basics; you can go back and fill in more details as you think of them.

Morning routine:
7:00 AM - 7:30 AM: Breakfast as a family
7:30 AM - 8:00 AM: School drop-off
8:30 AM - 3:00 PM: School hours
3:30 PM - 4:30 PM: Homework and study time
4:30 PM - 6:00 PM: Free play or structured extracurricular activities

Evening routine:
6:30 PM - 7:30 PM: Dinner as a family
7:30 PM - 8:00 PM: Bath time and bedtime preparations
8:00 PM - 8:30 PM: Bedtime story and cuddle time
8:30 PM: Lights out!

The Personal Touch
To make your parenting plan more meaningful, consider adding personal touches. You can include references to your favorite parenting books or inspirational quotes that resonate with your values and beliefs. These elements can serve as reminders of your guiding principles as parents.

As you embark on this journey of creating your PPP, remember that it's a living document. It should reflect your family's unique dynamics and adapt as your children grow and your circumstances change. Make it enjoyable to reference, and keep it updated to ensure it remains a valuable resource for your family's evolving needs.

Step 2 - Develop the Plan

Development

Define your mission and your vision clearly. Your mission will often be straightforward, like "keeping the baby safe and healthy." In contrast, your vision represents a long-term goal, such as "watching my children graduate from college and secure fulfilling careers."

For me, the mission was the cornerstone of my parenting plan. My primary goal was to ensure my baby remained healthy and safe. I understood that my personal choices needed to be thoughtful and avoid unnecessary risks. Protecting my child from danger was always my top priority. For example, I remember seeing a news story about a parent who placed their child dangerously close to a bear for a photo—something I would never consider doing.

At the same time, it's important to know when to step back. If a relative or friend did or said something to my child that I didn't entirely agree with, I learned to let it go if it wasn't harmful. New parents can benefit from listening courteously to advice from family and friends. There's no harm in hearing different perspectives, and you don't need to engage in arguments or debates over your parenting choices. Remember, you can consider their opinions without feeling obligated to follow them.

Make some notes about developing your approach.

_____

_____

_____

_____

Develop the Plan

Consider theses approaches:

- *The baby comes first* - I prioritized my baby's well-being by avoiding time-consuming or risky activities, understanding that maintaining my own health, rest, and support was essential to being the best, most purposeful parent I could be.
- *Provide structure and consistency* - I sought out reliable childcare by establishing routines, staying attentive to my child's demeanor, seeking recommendations, and thoroughly evaluating facilities, ensuring my baby felt secure and cared for while I balanced work and parenting responsibilities.
- *Stay mindful to manage your stress level* - I worked to manage my emotions and speak calmly instead of yelling, believing that maintaining control and setting a positive tone would teach my children healthier responses and improve our long-term relationship.
- *Be carful of the language you use* - I deliberately avoided using what I consider foul language at home to set a standard of appropriate speech, prevent embarrassing situations, and ensure my children understood what was acceptable behavior.
- *Reinforce the behavior you want your child to repeat* - I applied positive reinforcement to encourage good behavior and used careful language to differentiate acceptable actions from unacceptable ones, recognizing that reinforcing desired behavior is more effective than punishment.

NOTES:

Develop the Plan

Continued:

- *Communication and listening are essential* - Mastering effective communication and active listening, including maintaining eye contact, responding thoughtfully, and avoiding "baby talk," was essential to building a strong connection with my children and showing them how deeply they mattered to me.
- *Model acceptable behavior consistently* - Model the values and behaviors you want your children to learn by handling situations with respect, understanding, and calmness, teaching them how to navigate life's challenges and grow into adults you can be proud of.
- *Focus on how they feel about themselves* - It is crucial to nurture your child's self-esteem by understanding their thoughts, emphasizing their inner strengths over appearance, and helping them develop confidence, self-worth, and a strong sense of identity.
- *Delegate to others* - Recognizing my weaknesses, I delegated tasks like sex education and home-schooling to trusted individuals who were better equipped, allowing me to manage my limitations, reduce stress, and ensure my children received the best support possible.
- *Leave work stress at work* - Focus on your children when you get home, treating it as a joyful time to connect, ask about their day, and be fully present with them.

In uncertain moments, trust your judgment and the preparation behind your Purposeful Parenting Plan, knowing that your self-awareness and strengths will guide you to make the best decisions possible.

NOTES:

_____

_____

_____

_____

Notes

3. Execute the Plan

The following information will help prepare you for implementing the PPP. Putting in this pre-work will pay off in the end.

- **Be aware of defensiveness** - Being aware of defense mechanisms like projection, denial, displacement, and rationalization can help parents avoid unintentionally harmful behaviors and promote healthier, more effective parenting.
- **Avoid unacceptable behavior** - While we all have imperfections, managing avoidable behaviors—like intentionally irritating our children—can foster healthier, more positive parent-child relationships.
- **Minimize guilt and regret** - Guilt, a feeling of remorse for perceived wrongs, and regret, a sense of sadness over past actions, are natural emotions for parents, but your Purposeful Parenting Plan (PPP) aims to minimize these feelings by encouraging thoughtful decision-making, self-forgiveness, and learning from experiences rather than dwelling on past mistakes.
- **Let your children decide their future** - Parents should support their children's unique dreams and interests rather than projecting their own unfulfilled aspirations, ensuring children feel free to pursue their own paths without guilt or pressure.
- **Follow the plan** - The core of the purposeful parenting is creating a thoughtful, adaptable plan to address challenges by identifying concerns, committing to safety, and implementing creative solutions tailored to your child's needs and personality.
- **Review your PPP** - Regularly review and adapt your plan to meet your evolving family needs, maintaining consistency, staying organized, and embracing a positive mindset to navigate life's challenges, ensuring your plan becomes a natural part of your daily routine.
- **Make the plan consistent** - Reflect on what strengthens you as a parent, whether it's faith, prayer, or personal resilience, and draw on these sources to help you navigate the challenges of implementing your parenting plan.

NOTES:

Notes

4. Collect Feedback

The final step of the plan, collecting feedback, was an enlightening experience for me, and it was well worth it.

Give Yourself Feedback First
To measure your success as a parent, evaluate how effectively your parenting strategies are reflected in your children's development by focusing on the following key criteria:
- Career Alignment:
- Assess whether your children have chosen careers that align with their passions and interests.
- Behavior and Interaction:
- Observe how they interact with family members and peers—do they engage constructively, or are they argumentative?
- Life Enjoyment:
- Consider if they are finding joy and satisfaction in life, which reflects emotional well-being.
- Positive Traits:
- Look for signs of happiness, good citizenship, and a sense of responsibility in their daily actions.
- PPP Goals Realization:
- Reflect on whether the goals outlined in your Purposeful Parenting Plan (PPP) have been met.

Throughout the parenting journey, adapt your approach based on new situations and observe your children's behavior, achievements, and social interactions for continuous feedback. Encourage independence and assertiveness, ensuring they can voice their needs and make decisions confidently. Celebrate milestones, such as securing a mortgage or excelling in a career, as evidence of their growth and autonomy. These indicators, combined with their happiness and ability to navigate life's challenges, provide a comprehensive measure of your parenting success.

NOTES:

Collect Feedback

Children

To effectively discuss your parenting style with your children and gain valuable feedback, consider the following approach to foster openness and reflection:

- Create Opportunities for Dialogue:
- Schedule dedicated time to talk, such as video calls or in-person meetings, especially if your children live in different locations. This shows you value their input and are willing to listen.
- Ask Specific Questions:
- Explore which aspects of your parenting they found helpful or challenging, and whether they feel prepared for life's obstacles. Be curious and open-minded about their experiences.
- Encourage Candid Feedback:
- Foster a relaxed atmosphere filled with humor and warmth, allowing them to share honestly without fear of judgment or guilt.
- Reflect on Their Insights:
- Consider their feedback thoughtfully and recognize that each child may have different memories or perceptions of certain events. Use these insights to understand their unique experiences.
- Celebrate Their Achievements:
- Acknowledge how your parenting influenced their successes, such as personal confidence, professional accomplishments, and core values like respect, health, and community service.
- Stay Open to New Perspectives:
- Be willing to learn from their observations, even if it means discovering new terms or methods that align with your approach, like "Gentle Parenting."
- Affirm Your Connection:
- Reassure them that their thoughts matter, and highlight how these conversations deepen your relationship and demonstrate the lasting impact of your parenting.

By implementing these steps, you create a meaningful space for reflection, growth, and a deeper understanding of your parenting journey.

NOTES:

_____

_____

_____

_____

Collect Feedback

Grandchildren
When discussing your parenting style with your grandchildren, consider the following approach to foster understanding and meaningful dialogue:
- Ask for Their Perspective:
- Invite your grandchildren to share how they perceive you as a grandparent. Encourage them to be open and honest about their thoughts and feelings.
- Acknowledge Their Observations:
- Listen to their feedback, whether it's positive or constructive. For example, they might notice that you are organized, kind, or sometimes assertive.
- Reflect on How Your Traits Affect Them:
- Consider how your behaviors, such as being organized or encouraging assertiveness, impact their comfort level. Be receptive to their feelings if they express discomfort.
- Balance Encouragement with Sensitivity:
- If they feel uneasy about being pushed to take risks or work on weaknesses, adjust your approach to be supportive without being too assertive or "pushy."
- Adapt to Blended Family Dynamics:
- Recognize that grandchildren, especially in blended families, may not have experienced your full parenting style. Be mindful of their unique experiences and tailor your interactions accordingly.
- Show That You Value Their Feelings:
- Thoughtfully navigate these relationships by demonstrating that their perspectives matter. This helps create a harmonious and respectful family dynamic.

By using these strategies, you can maintain open communication and build stronger connections with your grandchildren.

NOTES:

Notes

Notes

Keep Going!

Hopefully, this workbook has served as a tool for you to collect your thoughts, jot down ideas, and formulate the beginnings of a play that you can follow throughout your parenting journey.

Of course you can decide to use this workbook alone, but you may want to pair it with other methods that allow for even more in-depth content. Remember, there's no one-size-fits-all approach; it should be something that resonates with you and fits your lifestyle. Here are some options to consider.

Journal: A journal is excellent for those who enjoy a more informal and narrative approach. You can record your thoughts, experiences, and observations as your parenting journey unfolds. It's a way to capture the emotional aspects of parenting along with practical details.

Notepad with Sections: If you prefer more structure, consider using a notepad with individual sections. Each section can focus on different aspects of your parenting plan, making finding and updating specific information easier.
Folder with loose pages: A folder with pages is a versatile choice for flexibility and longevity. You can add, remove, or rearrange pages as needed. This format is handy if you anticipate your plan evolving over time.

Tablet or smartphone: Many applications for taking notes can be useful for someone who uses their phone or tablet a lot and wants to jot things down quickly. Later, you can go back and clarify or organize your thoughts. You can also add alerts to remind you when it's time to update or review your plan.

Whatever you decide, continue to create a plan that you can update along the way. It should be a "living" document that adapts to each situation you encounter.

WANNA LEARN MORE?

For more detailed information, check out my book!
**Was It Worth It?
How to Create Your Own Purposeful Parenting Plan**

Here's to purposeful parenting

and an amazing journey!